The Body Remembers

Maureen Sherbondy

UNSOLICITED
PRESS
PORTLAND, OREGON
SINCE 2012

Attention schools and businesses: for discounted copies on large orders, please contact the publisher directly.

For information contact:
Unsolicited Press
Portland, Oregon
www.unsolicitedpress.com
orders@unsolicitedpress.com
619-354-8005

Cover Design: Kathryn Gerhardt
Editor: Kristen Marckmann

ISBN: 978-1-963115-53-6

Acknowledgments

"Body" and "After Surgery" appeared in *13ʰ Moon*

"Sutra" appeared in *Feminist Studies*

"Sacrifice" and "Rash" appeared in *RiverSedge*

"Fold" and "Thread" appeared in the chapbook *The Year of Dead Fathers*

"Sculpture: Mother & Child" appeared in *California Quarterly*

"Wreck Collection" appeared in *Pennsylvania English*

"Helping the Self at Eight," "Toward Drowning," and "Rash" appeared in the chapbook *Weary Blues*

"Roses" appeared in *Hole in the Head Review*

"When We Lose Both Parents" appeared in *Off the Coast*

"Hunger" appeared in the anthology *The Sound of Poets Cooking*

"Going Home" appeared in *Broad River Review*

"Circuitry" appeared in *Jelly Bucket*

"Cousins I Never Met" appeared in *Connotation Press*

"Taschlich" appeared in *European Judaism*

"Laundry Rant" appeared in *Icon*

"At the Mikveh, Age 4" appeared in *Zeek*

"Tikkun Olam, the Dream, and the Thread" appeared in *Poetica*

"Losing Jersey" appeared in the Raleigh *News & Observer*

"Ocean Lullaby" appeared in *Cairn*

"Gone Fishing on the River Styx" appeared in *Redheaded Stepchild*

"Excision" (previously called "Removal") appeared in *Lynx Eye*

"Captain von Trapp in the Surgical Suite" appeared in *North Carolina Literary Review*

"The Speculum" appeared in *Talking River Review*

"Killing Time in the Waiting Room" appeared in *New York Quarterly*

Table of Contents

DROWNING

SUTRA

"At night I closed my eyes and saw my bones threading the mud of my grave."

—Jack Kerouac

Body

Once again this body
seems not like my own,
just some pea pod waiting
to be shucked away.

My body keeps taking over
these poems. Body opens,
nature comes in.

Body wants
to be cut away.

I am trying to find the peas inside.

During labor my first baby
couldn't find his way out. He twisted
his neck back towards darkness,
the waiting light too strong
for his new eyes.
The doctor got the scalpel.
Did I ever have a choice?

They sliced into my numbed-pear middle
as if I were not even there.
I saw small, wet feet rise
out of me.
They stapled me shut.

How could I not have separated body
from mind? How can I ever own
this body again?

Now it wants to open back up,
pull in the outside for good,
now that the body is closed,
now that it is too late.

Sutra

She is slicing
a golden apple
into slivers, when
edge of jagged metal
meets peachy flesh.

Red blood leaks out—
warm, bright.
She takes a breath,
exhales. So this is
the life inside of self.
This is the passion
she has been hoarding,
hiding.

Before she interrupts
the flow with cotton cover,
a fine silver thread
exits from cut flesh,
moves snakelike
into the air, stretched-out
accordion filling the room
with music of life, silver notes.

It pulls itself the length
of the kitchen, finds an open
window, travels west, floating
with the outside air.

The girl stares, left there
with air-soaked cut
transforming to scab,
opening closed.

The Speculum

The speculum is cold
but necessary. I am trying
to make sense of love
arising inside disease.

How many times must
I be peeled open?
Am I an orange?
Am I a can of paint?
The doctor speaks
in terms of fruit
and objects like golf balls.
There are numbers
in centimeters that carry
no weight in my body.
Parts expand that should not
grow. I do not know how to shrink.

Once a man entered
my home. I invited him
in. It was dark here
and my head got lost
in malignant clouds for too long.

Such a toxic city of blood and waste.

Inside, my girly body glowed warm. A blanket.
A cocoon. Alice's found
hole in the ground after the long red rain.
Others, too, grew lost inside.
This amused me to no end. Prince of Jacks.
King of deception.
There were no clocks in the dark place.
At some point
I threw a never-ending party.
Liquor bottles, jazz, too many
dance cards. I pick you and you
and you.

Until the door slammed shut
and the adult voice woke up.

But now instruments
have become my lovers.
Cold, brutal arms and hands.
Someone has opened up
a lemonade stand inside
my body. There is no lemonade,
only a plush lawn growing thicker
named *uterus*. Named *keep it coming*.

In real life, I remain composed. I knew
one day I'd lose control. There is
a woman screaming
with a megaphone—
Keep it coming!

Inside filled with disease,
growing cells that should
not grow. I yell, *I am done*
with making human beings.
Who gave you permission
to bury aliens inside me?
Don't even get me started
on buildings of prayer and God.

Old home for my three sons.
Seeds planted, grown to trees.
Warm cradle created by me
and my mother and my mother's mother.

Do not speak to me with your silver
tongue. Steel thief of endometrium.
Enemy. Helper. Look for the helpers,
I told my children. Such disguises

they wear. Men in white uniforms.
Still, I need you like I need
a strong body on top of these hips.

Stop prying me open.

Dark creatures hide inside.
The ones from my childhood
closet. But pry me open. I need to know.

In the surgical suite,
the uniformed men
say, *Close your eyes, Sleeping Beauty.*
You trust no one holding sharp-edged blades.

Instrument with no song.
No string or bow. How will I
hear music again? Now just
these notes of despair
released from my own
fleshy mouth.
Bring on the chorus.
Excise those dark places.

Intersection

A single thread rests in my hand,
one end grasped by my younger fingers.
Soon, items cling to the other end,
a hanging mobile of sorts—
that found blue feather,
a stone I held up to the sun
and witnessed clarity,
that first earned dollar bill,
later paychecks, love notes,
a wedding band, birth photos,
the three houses we lived in.
Your thread crossed mine
at some point in time, tangled
up my life. I want it back—
my past, my present, my given name.
If I cut away the intersecting
string, will I fall and lose it all
or return to the very beginning?

Water

The rain locates no escape
so it accumulates on macadam.
Concrete barriers prevent exodus,
so you try not to hydroplane
into the other lane. If only
the car were a boat, you'd simply
float away from danger. Somehow
you remain unscathed.

Consider the body, too,
is mostly water. Liquid
that both sustains and drowns.
Without it, you would be
only bones and skin, organs.

Isn't everything then
about the body?
Before that first breath came,
you swam in a fleshy pool
until the water broke,
releasing you in nakedness
not yet knowing how to
finesse a course
through this arid universe.

After Surgery

When she woke, her arms swirled
around the room like spokes
on a wheel. She swatted at nothing
and everything, trying to slap
and poke everyone and no one.
In fun, the nurses joked, *She's a wild one.*

What floated, hung in the sterile air,
they could not see this dark menagerie,
unraveled only by a patient in an altered
fighting state. It would not dissipate.
Latent animals released from twilight sleep
while she shut her eyes to pain and light,
drug-gas singing through her fleshy abode.

What slipped out of mind's dark walls,
escaping from intubated throat, while straps
arrested her against surgery gurney?
They could not compress everything
that loomed and drifted in the room.

The Lady Who Swatted Flies

First, the opossum
scurrying about the garage,
shadows,
light steps rushing away.

Dreams gnawed open
by silhouettes
until hands intervened,
ending all scurrying.

She had no choice
but to serve those green pellets
that created a burst of thirst
to death's shadow.

Then flies appeared,
swarm of dark-legged nuisances,
flitting reminders of her own actions.
She swatted them. They came faster
than she swatted, so she sprayed poison
towards the shadow.

Then, this morning
that black bird in the closed garage.
Flying shadow.
Perhaps the bird would eat the flies?
That song playing in her head:
There was an old lady who swallowed
a fly . . .

Her mouth opens,
invites them in—
the flies, the bird, the shadow.

C-section Scar

The throbbing begins ten years later
whenever my son falls down at camp
or bumps his arm against a pole at school.

That shut window from where he reached
out to the world, swells and reddens
as if a small messenger were left behind

like a telephone line to ring in his pain.

Fold

She folds her cards.
She folds a blanket,
then her legs, her arms, her body
into a square.
She fits easily everywhere.
Fleshy napkin, placemat,
welcome mat.
But after a while she grows
bored as a board
and folds herself out to sea
letting the water carry her,
letting her folded-self drift
before opening up into a sail
to propel her body forward
in the wind.

Return Policy

During the divorce proceedings
the cuckolded husband demands,
I want my kidney back!
His wife says no, she's moved on.

He wants his heart back too;
it's damaged now, or completely
gone. He's amazed he can even
stand or work. At night he wakes
to absence.

Her side of the bed empty, waiting
for a change of heart, a loyal
kidney prodding from afar,
Go home.

His back aches. He places a hand
where that kidney once rested,
calls out to the lost organ and to her,
Come back, both of you.

It was a match, a miracle.
What were the odds?

1/800,000 or greater.
He saw it as a sign,
thought it meant love
was fated to last 'til death.

But no, it only meant she'd live
another thirty years
by someone else's side.
His kidney content inside
her body, sleeping
beside her new lover.

The Party at Night

There is a party every evening
above the trees; that is why
we do not hear the birds singing
after darkness. They are flitting about
over the universal dance floor,
sipping champagne from silver-flask
feeders while star-lit strobe lights
flash about the primordial ballroom.

Sometimes our bodies float
from our dreams
and travel to the party.
We wake, hungover
with desire, naked
beneath our morning sheets.

Old Sanctuary

So what does one do
when danger lies within
the sanctuary?

Here, invisible gardeners
dispersing small spores plant cysts
inside this once-fertile soil.

No flower garden
can rise in the dark room.
How does one reach inside
and pull out lethal weeds?

O holy place where I once
sought refuge of silence and safety—
you have set a trap
destroying me from the inside out.

Removal

1.

And what if each organ
is connected like pieces in Jenga?
When the doctor removes one section,
other segments collapse into each other
to disperse loosely across the body's
ocean. Maybe the surgeon could insert
a replica like a missing shelf inset,
support beam for what used to be
part of me, to confuse the cervix
into believing the foundation remains
intact. Like a headstone standing in
for the person once the body has passed.

2.

Building on stilts remains
even though the ocean's waving hands
have pushed one pole away
from the house to tilt
the foundation. The house bends
now, unable to stand upright

and certain. Those uneven floors
slant, cause every person to falter and fall.

3.

When the roots of a tree die,
what becomes of trunk
and limbs? O uterus, cradle
for three sons, holder of secrets,
who will I be without you?

Tender of Land

Never a gardener, I am
at a loss when wandering
this thick patch of empty sacs,
discarded cradle beds.
No dirt here, just cells
and the outline of hollow bulbs.

Who planted these tubers?
Derelict tender of my land. Now
this landscape in demise has grown
wild with futile weeds. Might I
lift a dandelion, blow
its cottony wisps with a wish
toward a certain future?

My father taught me to cultivate
rosebushes. He pointed to
stems and thorns.
But what do men know
about a woman's garden?

Fool that you were at eight,
you believed tomorrow's roses meant

love, romance. But that same man
rubbed daily thorns across
my mother's flesh until she bled.

Those roses have turned black
in the dying hour before departure,
and those thorns that once found
my mother's skin
now reside within my own corpus halls.

Captain von Trapp in the Surgical Suite

It's Christopher Plummer in surgical scrubs
holding a guitar instead of a scalpel.
I tell him his version of "Edelweiss"
is a favorite memory from my youth,
that every man I later dated was held up
to him in that one glowing moment
and no one has compared to Captain von Trapp.

My present husband sings karaoke
even though he lacks the voice;
it takes a certain kind of man to belt out lyrics
out of tune and in front of an audience.

Christopher Plummer is about to remove
my uterus. I tell him I have terrible doubts
about his skill as a surgeon. Just because
a person is talented in one arena doesn't mean
that ability spreads to other areas like medicine.

Trust me, he says. The infusion into my veins
is a bottle of my favorite gin. Feeling woozy,
I shrug, realizing I no longer control either body
or life. Before falling under, I recall reading

that "Edelweiss" was dubbed in by another singer.
Is the illusion of talent just as good as the real thing?

Too late to change doctors, I fade
in the clean, white room, seeing star-like flowers rising
as "Edelweiss" carries across the gurney
and my uterus dances away from my body.

Rash

I wake to a burst of rash
in bloom across my torso;
red bumps, ridges
beneath breasts and armpits,
rosy confetti on my hips.

Caged behind the cold-pressed
bars of dreams—is this the way
songs and secrets leave
the body when imprisoned
for too long?

Yesterday, someone held a palm
against my lips. Words back-flowed
along my tongue, nowhere to go
but down again, choking
me through day and night.

In the mirror, these raised bumps
like sore eyes stare back at me.
Yards of swollen lips eclipse silence;
red rage tries to surface from the body
to let that song, those secrets, out again.

The Cracking

Desiring nourishment
I cracked a single egg.
Instead of yolk and albumen,
out fell a straw-hued golden
thread. Rising up, it connected to the sky.

I tugged at golden filament; out came a farm—
a hen, a goat, a horse, a barn,
a bale of hay, all floated through my kitchen.

Taken before its live emerging,
the shelled memory still
thriving, that chick drifted
about my eggless kitchen.

Body Canvas

Someone draws on my hand;
flesh disappears.
Am I canvas?
Am I
at all?
Blue ink stares back.
I am sky.
I color my body
with feathers.
Body vanishes.
I fly.

Killing Time in the Waiting Room

Count the hospital ceiling tiles.
Try to recall the names of doctors
you've met. Listen in on conversations of other
worried families in the waiting room.
Determine whose loved one is most likely to survive
and most likely to die. Memorize the announcements
over the PA system; repeat them two hours from now.
Recall the last conversation between
you and your father. Was it really about
the stock market? How relevant is the decline
in the stock market at this moment
on a scale of one to ten?
How often are the floors mopped?
Do they use Lysol or bleach?
Try to determine the name of the disease
or illness that will land you here in thirty
years; smile at people who pass by,
then count how many smile back.
Mouth a prayer. Contemplate
the existence of God
and the importance of science.

MEMORY

"Happiness is nothing more than good health and a bad memory."

—Albert Schweitzer

Does the Body Remember?

Does skin have memory,
like how my car knows
my seat position
when I unlock the doors?

If you arrived at my door today,
twenty years since I last saw you,

if you pressed a hand
against my face
(my eyes closed),
would my skin,
my heart start up again?

The warm flash of you
setting aflame my flesh.

Becoming a Tree

Tree roots found
a woman's ankles,
threaded around her
thin, skinned bones.

She woke, merged
with the tree's bark,
the rings of the trunk
filling her lungs
with ancient stories.

A year later, the roots
released her wiser self.
She wandered back home
with a thousand tales
upon her tongue.

Carved

How content she was
as part of that tree—her house, her roots,
the possibilities waiting out there,
sights unfolding before her eyes,
blue jays, red cardinals of chance
visiting her outstretched arms.

A man comes, let's call him Geppetto
(or Bob or Fred).
He wants a puppet,
takes axe to bark, cuts down
the tree, roots and all.
He cradles a perfect block
of magic wood, brings it back
to his shop
        chop   chop.

All the things she should have been,
could have been,
        sawed away:
musician, chef, philanthropist,
the list goes on and on.
Once cut, it's gone,

that unformed pulp, potential
chipped away, abandoned on the floor
with sawdust.

She had taken vows not to lie
or cheat. The master wrote these words
for her; she repeated them
when ordered to.
(Hadn't all the others?)

Soon he grew
bored with the puppet
he had made, tossed it
                           aside,
went back to the woods
to find a different tree
to cut and carve into a puppet bride.

Now this old piece
of wood in the corner
is stuck for good
in the silly shape of a puppet
and can't figure out
how to carve herself back
to what she had been before.

Inbox

Once again, some stranger in a foreign country
delivers offerings; typed messages appear
in my mailbox: three-inches growth promised.
Please her, make her scream. Sexy videos for download.
Take her breath away. And it does
take away my breath. My fingers tremble
on the keyboard, poised and waiting,
the shock of blunt sentences assaulting
my eyes. I wonder if nuns use computers
and if they do, are these unheavenly
notes sent to their boxes too? Or is there a list:
Do not send to? What cyber search did I input
to end up at the receiving end of this?
Once, a picture appeared—
a giant throbbing penis sliding between
a virtual stranger's lips. I could not look away.
Frozen for a moment, I eventually pressed delete.
That night while I slept, my mind received
yet another download, a giant penis throbbing
inside my dreams, no delete key in sight.

Laundry Rant

On the way to do yet another load of laundry,
you see a lone shoe and hat in the middle of the room
and fear your kids will fall, topple towards danger,
so you stoop down and lift the items from the path, then ponder
garden paths, that arboretum in Arcadia, California,
and wonder why you have not visited a single garden
in twenty years. Imaginary flowers dry up and die
on the carpet path, and you can't recall where
you were going, so you busy your hands and tidy up—
plump the pillows, tuck in couch covers, bury thoughts
in coverings, in hats on cold heads,
hats on that boy in college who looked like Richard Gere
merged with David Byrne. He wore hats in winter
in Jersey and you wonder where he is now.
You recall how he removed that hat in bed and said,
You are dri-ving me ab-so-lute-ly cra-zy
in that slow, low voice. Beneath the swirling scent
of floral laundry softener and tolling music of loud rolling
dryer drum, you feel warm, tingly. Twenty years later
and you can't recall why you broke up
and wonder if he's married and if so, does his wife forget
where she is going and get lost on the way to the laundry room,
the gardens of the past vine-winding their way into the present.

Excision

Behind my cousin's eye
they find a sac, a cyst,
decide to excise it.

The doctor dissects
this body mystery.
He finds a tooth, a hair.
How long had it been there?
What was this cyst? Lost twin
absorbed after cell division.

My odd cousin. Always quiet,
uneasy. I blamed it on the accident,
that Mack Truck going fifty,
his dented bones and skin.

He retreated to a hospital bed
for a year, from four to five.
Relatives were amazed he was even alive.
At night, he was perturbed
by the shake-rumble of passing vehicles,
a whisper heckling inside his ears.

Maybe he knew what tried to grow
inside of him but never could. At night
the unborn twin fed distressing secrets
from that prison-head. Did he ask:
Why you instead of me?

Losing Jersey

On the phone from New Jersey
my mother declares with a laugh,
You're beginning to sound Southern!
I flinch, shake my head no no no
to the empty room in my Raleigh home.

No, I am not! I reply, verbal arsenal ready
to spout a repertoire of denial.
Ten years spent here—I swore across
state lines it would not happen.

When you said daawg, just now.
My heart races through the possibility of change.
The question, how could this have happened
to me? Jersey girl who used to listen
to Springsteen, spend summers at the shore:
Asbury, Belmar, Long Beach Island.

Sure, I've surrounded myself with Southern
friends from towns with names I can't pronounce
(Fuquay-Varina, Salisbury, Beaufort).

I have listened to them talk, admired the slow
molasses way their tongues caress words
before releasing phrases into the Southern air. But emulation?

I quickly try to prove her wrong, let out a song
of words sure to show my birth origin (Metuchen).
Coffee, awful, I nervously ramble on.

The Jersey's gone is her reply, no trace of it
evident now. Jersey fading from the telephone line
like static heard then gone. An empty echo of loss
replacing any accent on my Carolina tongue.

At the Mikveh, Age Four

For weeks my brothers flooded me
with tales of drowning,
said the special pool was where
young girls sank
and did not rise again.

When we appeared at the mikveh—
attempt to quell the swell
of non-Jewish blood swimming
through our veins—
I planted myself upon a bench
refusing to budge from my position

wanting to live no matter
the future cost. In my heart
I was a Jew, this I knew,
no ceremony could make it so.

Better to stay than to go.
While brothers and mother
vanished under water

and prayers rang out in the other rooms,
alone I remained, wordless, prayerless,
still and silent as a stone.

Tashlich

I cut the fish,
lift fleshy pink
sliver to my lips.

How many sins
have you swallowed,
dead salmon?

Jews toss
transgressions
into the water.

Breadcrumbs of infidelity.
Pebbles of lies.
Pocket dust of indifference.

I chew and swallow,
hope my body
stays free

from what
I have
eaten.

How do we live
with our sins
that return—

a small pebble
caught in the back
of our throat.

(Note: Tashlich refers to a ceremony in which sins are cast out by
throwing them into a body of water.)

Tikkun Olam, the Dream, and the Thread

He reclines inside my dream,
his eyes neither opened nor closed.
The Hebrew book
in his lap, pages set flat.

I move closer, lean in.
His fingers rest on two words:
tikkun olam.
What message, Opa?
I spend the morning
paging through possibility.

Repair of the world,
or mend the fissures
inside my own self?
So many cracks lately,
visible even from the heavens.

A month later the towers
crack, tremble, fall.
Smoke remains in my eyes.

Is this what the messenger
sent, what was meant by those words
delivered from the dead?

Yesterday at a party,
a ceramic fondue pot split
in two; chocolate avalanche
suffocated the flame.

Today I place a roasting pan
inside the oven; soft cracking
alerts my ears. The pan is split
in half, like land after a quake,
sudden separation between past
and future. The danger of falling in
stares back at me.

Where are those seamstresses
when you need them?

Again, I ask, what does it mean?

I look to the night sky for answers, to the stars
and blackness and moon. Inside my chest
I feel the knot of thread pulling, rising.
When I open my mouth, a silver thread

deserts me, searching for the hole
of the silver needle.

Where are the hands that know how to sew?
The silent, still hands of the dead
can no longer weave the earth together again
unless they know how to rise inside our dreams
and gently guide our hands, needle by needle,
thread by thread, fissure by fissure, seam by seam.

Cousins I Never Met

Fire burns down the entire forest
but still one flower thrives. The moon's
silhouette against the sky reminds me
yes, we are still alive. We ran and walked
through yesterday's parade. You thought
the kite you ran with on the sand
could fly up to the night-imprisoned moon.
My cousins, too, (all gone too soon) watched this same light
in Germany as night-time, day-time prisoners in
rooms fit for two or three, not fifty.

Two years ago we let go of white balloons
at the newborn's funeral. Five days
he lived. Son, nephew, brother. Five days. We looked up
until white globes blurred into white clouds.
Devoured. We throw rocks at death both now
and then. Still, death stays with you and me
hours, months, through years of lingering. Remember

painting the German Shepherd thick
with tomato juice to release the stink.
Oh, that stink, it lingers. Oh, this scent
of death, too. Stink of burning flesh,

I have heard about it, read about it.
Lampshade flesh, they whisper in the halls.

Now walk with me inside
the burned-down forest, take in the sweet
perfume of one flower reaching up
to the sun and moon. My relatives made it
through until the final hours and then
and then. Auschwitz, final hour. The end
when release could be tasted, sulphur burning
on his defeated tongue. Führer fury. The end arrived
when release could be swallowed from the air
so close, and yet. Their blood, our blood waters
burnt soil. We plant new seeds. We march forward.

Leading Prayer at Hebrew School

My turn, the only girl
in class. I stand at the front
of the room;
nine sets of dark eyes
stare, goading until
the streak of red
flares across my cheeks.
They incite the tripping
of Hebrew words and trope.
My goal: to chant clearly
from *baruch* to *amen*
without stumble or pause.
Two boys compose silly faces
attempting to make me
falter between *bless*
and *God.* I block them out
just as I do years later
when the bullies try
to make me cry.

DROWNING

"If you cannot get rid of the family skeleton, you may as well make it dance."

—George Bernard Shaw

Toward Drowning

Years ago, my family
began their slow descent
toward drowning. I paddled
my hands as fast as possible,
but my brothers, my mother,
even that distant father
kept pulling me under
the known surface.

Pursued daily by piranhas,
those teeth
nipping away at fleshy youth,
and the constant sting
of jellyfish poverty. I asked for help
but my mother was deaf, off
performing her synchronized
swim routine, dating her turnstile
of men; as one left, another floated in.
Mother, I am sinking,
I yelled. She did not hear me.

In my dead-child's-float,
dreams were seagulls

gliding above with their hopeful
plumes. Sometimes a single
feather descended inside my hand
and I'd clutch it for months.

I finally swam away, lifted
my water-wrinkled feet from the waves,
found an island, warm-sand
sanity. Sanctuary.

At night I wake,
saltwater and silt spilling
from tongue and dreams.
No one appears to save me.

There are only stars
and my own flailing fingers.

When voices carry
across the waves, I listen
but vigilantly watch
for those ghost crabs
to appear, pinching
my toes, trying to pull me back
into that deep, cold ocean again.

Family Fabric

Years spent stitching
these swatches onto
the children's bodies—
swatch of knowledge,
square of kindness.

After they leave,
that dangling thread
connected to our little finger
tugs at us day and night.

Fabric piece designed
of our own flesh
leaves so little left of us.

Helping the Self at Eight

I reach for her;
it is thirty years earlier—
she can't yet see me.

She is covering her face
with a pillow, covering her ears
with small hands.

Don't make it your problem!
I tell her, hovering.
Your parents are wacko, immature.

They don't see the damage yet.
This isn't about you.
I try to shake her.

Get out while you can.
Confront them, wedge
your body between them.

I try. I try to protect her,
to pull her out
so years later she will know

it isn't her fault.
Every time a man yells,
raises his voice to her,

she won't retreat
to that pink-girl room
with lace curtains,

place a pillow over her head.
I try, but cannot reach her.
I cannot be seen

by those eyes
that keep turning away
from myself.

Hunger

I teach my children survival
to ensure continuation of name and line,
show how even a poor person can sustain
life on makeshift meals found in every café
and fast food establishment.

How condiments of mustard, ketchup,
mayonnaise squeezed out like packaged
caviar onto unwrapped saltine crackers
can create a square sandwich piled tower high,
yellow, red, and white globs dripping and oozing
between stiff, salty layers.

That the fancy foreign car dealership
stocks juice, soda, and dozens of glistening
glazed doughnut delights for their clientele
to devour. Lint in our pockets today, dollars
may follow tomorrow.

In my childhood kitchen
where bare refrigerator shelves held little—
ketchup, bread, milk, and eggs—
I learned these lessons too.

Make do with what there is,
create and stack dreams
from what there is not.

Wreck Collection

I recall the wreck moving—
brown woodie wagon
shedding rims, hubcaps
like body parts.

Missing front teeth
we sat open grin to open grin,
three brothers and I in the back seat,
teasing knee to knee,
my own knobby caps
scraped, scabbed over.

Dad in the driver's seat,
Mom leaning away
so far it seemed
she'd get sucked out
or fly, voluntarily as a bird,
through the rolled-down window.

The air pushing her
dark beehive hair away
from the bees and road
signs towards us.

That shocked look stagnant
in her locked eyes. One question
over and over:
How did I get here?

I, alone, noticed
between giggles
and rest stops
and too-quick lane changes.
I noticed so many parts
abandoned on the long road.

So many words not said
flying out of the car.

I noticed the silence,
the too-large space
between them,

his eyes set forward
toward a faraway place
that I couldn't yet see.

In her eyes, that gaze
traveling into the thick woods

searching for something
behind the evergreens,
something beyond this car,
this family, that I could not
see or touch or know.

Ocean Lullaby

The child remembers sound—
the swishing, splashing within,
back then, in that first ocean—
jellyfish-sac.

Later, far away,
sand between his toes and days,
those female voices
send for him.
Come back!
they sing.

As his feet corkscrew
into the sand,
ocean voices pulling at him
with each returning wave,
he knows.

He wants to go back
to where he began.

Gone Fishing on the River Styx

I convince the ferryman to let me
fish while we glide across the lilted current.

He shrugs and says, *You can't eat
when dead.* I cast the line anyway,

watch the leaden sinker lowering.
The bobbin floats, dives toward silt.

I flout my smelt and shad before his eyes
void of any appetite. While traveling, I slit

the fish, then swallow every morsel down
to show how hunger still remains, confounds

long after heart and brain have lapsed.

The Waiting

Charon, I am waiting
patiently for your boat
while waves from
the River Styx
lap against a mixture
of dirt and stones.

Shall I return back home
a fortnight, set a bird
in the oven, bread on a plate?

Perhaps light a fire
with warped wood
cut from an old boat,
while the hours grow late?

Will there be a siren warning
before departure?
Will the Israelites remove
the bloody mark from my door?

Charon, I grow tired waiting
for your boat. Let me sleep

awhile before the fire's heat
so sweet dreams might float
like water against this final night.

Early Tales

Your tongue hems in stories
heard at five and six.
The old woman
in the shoe,
the brother and sister
sent away to the woods.

Tales crawl out
decades later.
When you have
so many children,
you don't know
what to do but distract
and entertain them.

You turn to hoarding food
because of fears
of being abandoned.
Cans and boxes are stacked
neatly in your giant pantry.

In the dance that time delivers
to your floor, you confuse

early childhood truth
with those stories read
in bed by your own
neglectful parents.

Roses

My dead father still asks
for forgiveness. Years later
I set my own bushes in the yard,
watch as leaflets emerge
and thorns rise from the skin.

I recall him guiding my hands
to cut back the rose stems.
Each year we gathered
yellow, pink, and red
flowers, carried them inside.

Now I nourish these bushes
instead of dark rooms
of anger, instead of those
big hands punching walls,
instead of palms slapping
my mother's face.

Here are my father's hands in the garden
guiding my own grown hands.
He says, *Like this, do it this way.*
I remember the vase of roses

we set on the pine table
lighting up the house for days.

The Witch Speaks

Today the witch finds a way
to my tongue. I was half asleep
and she listened in on a call
from my mother.

(Oh, careful editor in my head,
why do you choose to abandon
me at such times?)

Before I could stop her,
the fire match of ire began.
Not familiar with the language
of tact or forgiveness,
that witch listed all missteps, insults,
and wrongs committed by traders.

A war began with smoky gossip and cruelty.

You are not yourself today,
my mother lashed back,
snapping me from my slumber.
I threw apologies across
the minefield. Too late.

Words like fire can destroy
two houses, can reach across entire states.
I thought that witch was crushed
by a house tossed asunder in a tornado,
but clever girl, she slipped away.

Circuitry

As if an electrician stands by
the light plate playing jokes,
someone is monkeying with
my mother's wiring, causing
intermittent firing and misfiring.

She's afraid the circuitry will fry
completely, cause a permanent
blackout as destiny. Sometimes
it smells like smoke in her house,
she tells me when I check on her.

All I recall are positives and negatives,
colored wires and batteries,
the instructions lost, unread
from that science lab kit
received for an early birthday.

I could never get the bulb to light up
as the box photo indicated it should.
My hands and brain became tangled.
Once, my brother took apart
my mini-bank slot machine.

Before he dissected it, when three
bars lined up, quarters would spill
into the metal tray. Curious boy,
he said he'd discover how
the wires made the money release.

He never put it back together again.
It sat sadly on my dresser, metal innards
and plastic parts. I picture my mother's
chambers right now. A tiny man flicking
the light switch on and off.

Her heart racing, then slowing down.
Wires twist, incite misfiring.
She wakes every morning
hoping to hit the jackpot, for light
to spill into her eyes for one more lucky day.

The Clown Painting

For years I wondered about the happy clown
painting that hung on the wall in our
split-level New Jersey home. Puzzled
that it didn't match the abstract art or decor
in other rooms. Out of place, it seemed.

My mother finally confided she'd created it.
Paint-by-number, she confessed,
finished after three tedious months
confined to bedrest. *I was bored
out of my mind*, she added.

She described how the placenta separated
in month six of her pregnancy. Bleeding.
Fear of the baby's death. Anxiety led
her hands to seek an outlet, so she moved
paint with brush across the canvas.

With each connected dot, she imagined making whole
that child within her body, visualized small hands clinging
to uterus walls. Hoping when that framed clown
decorated the living room, her child would live to see
it there, wearing a paint-by-number smile across his face.

Going Home

When we return home,
we walk backwards.
By the time we reach
the front door,
we are children again.

Our parents call us
in for supper
by those names
we long before
threw into the river.

Squabbles between siblings
start by dusk with tiny hands
punching and scratching
over that last cookie
or who won at Parcheesi.

The morning we leave,
we gain twelve inches
in height and decades of wisdom.
By the time we reach
our adult homes,
scratches are barely visible.

When We Lose Both Parents

We become grown
orphans again

O, stork
O, Great Sky Hand

Drop me again
inside a home
of cradling arms

Young Oliver,
all of us

Waiting open-mouthed
so hungry

Our mothers and fathers
taking with them

All the serving spoons
inside the house

Thread

Your ears are covered in dust, and I am
finally voicing what needs release. For years,
I opened my mouth, but no sound came free.

My tongue was frozen, stitched, and sewed
to my lip. Today, a bird lands on my windowsill
and I can't stop yapping.

Father, you can't take that thread with you.
The day your body flipped beneath cold dirt,
I found these scissors, cut loose those seams.

Sacrifice

In medieval Europe, it was widely believed that the pelican fed its
young on its own blood . . .

                    —*Birding*, A Nature Company Guide

I, too, have been the pelican mother,
poking holes through feathered skin,
releasing warm, thin blood as food
when there was none.

Was it not expected of me?
How else could I satiate these winged
offspring who gazed at me, waiting
in that beaks-open state?

There was no one else
to give what was needed.
Don't get me wrong—
I wanted all of them.
It's just this: I thought that sticks
and grass and fish would do.

Did not foresee that in the end
these holes would be so necessary,

leaving little left of me.
Who knew that self-mutilation alone
could satisfy their young cries?
Not I.

Sculpture: "Mother & Child"

Mother sanded that rock
for months, rubbing away
its roughness
with raw-skinned hands.
She wanted to smooth it out
like her own life,
to take hard stone,
shape it into something
polished and new.

In the basement she stayed
sanding day and night,
scouring through darkness,
pushing her way through light.
Pain pressing into her face, her palms,
her fingers, her joints. Remnants
of stone thrown into sink.

One day the stone split in two;
it caused her to pause,
then she polished that one too,
called them Mother & Child
when she was through.

And I knew through her bleeding knuckles

that two polished rocks can form

from one

so broken in two.

About the Author

Maureen Sherbondy's poems have appeared *in Southern Humanities Review, Feminist Studies, Calyx, New York Quarterly,* and other journals. She has won the Hart Crane Memorial Poetry Contest, the North Carolina Poet Laureate prize, and many other awards. Her most recent poetry books are *Lines in Opposition, Dancing with Dali,* and *The Art of Departure.* Sherbondy holds an MFA from Queens University of Charlotte. She resides in Durham, North Carolina.

About the Press

Unsolicited Press is based out of Portland, Oregon and focuses on the works of the unsung and underrepresented. As a womxn-owned, all-volunteer small publisher that doesn't worry about profits as much as championing exceptional literature, we have the privilege of partnering with authors skirting the fringes of the lit world. We've worked with emerging and award-winning authors such as Amy Shimshon-Santo, Brook Bhagat, Elisa Carlsen, Tara Stillions Whitehead, and Anne Leigh Parrish.

Learn more at unsolicitedpress.com. Find us on Instagram, X, Facebook, Pinterest, Bsky, Threads, YouTube, and LinkedIn. Unsolicited Press also writes a snarky newsletter on Substack.